Bible Women
of China

Paul Estabrooks

Open Doors

Sovereign World

Scripture quotations are taken from
The Holy Bible, New International Version.
© Copyright 1973, 1978, 1984 International Bible Society.
Used by permission.

ISBN: 1 85240 134 6

SOVEREIGN WORLD LIMITED
P.O. Box 777, Tonbridge, Kent TN11 0ZS, England.

Typeset and printed in the UK by Sussex Litho Ltd, Chichester, West Sussex.

Foreword

Just recently I had the privilege of meeting Sister Alice, whose story is in this booklet. When I think of her, I am reminded of the account of Hannah in the Bible. Just like Hannah, Alice had a personal adversary who taunted her almost every day to give up her faith, divorce her husband and adopt an easier lifestyle. She felt keenly the persecution that came her way. But she did not succumb.

Even whilst she was praying, Hannah was persecuted and accused of being drunk. But her life changed when she spoke with God.

I am sure that this is the secret of victory in the Persecuted Church. Alice was conscious of being heard by God. Today there is victory in her walk and victory in her face, even though her husband was imprisoned for over 21 years.

Now she works with her husband in a flourishing house church in Beijing, and together they are rejoicing that the "Man-child," Christ, is being formed in the local Church.

Read on, there's more…

Johan Companjen
President
Open Doors International

Introduction

"Many women were there, watching from a distance. They had followed Jesus from Galilee to care for his needs."

(Matthew 27:55)

The New Testament records the fact that many women were among the larger body of disciples that followed and served Jesus Christ. Unfortunately, we only know the names and stories of a few. We do know they were more loyal to Jesus at the time of his crucifixion than his male disciples. Despite the patriarchal society of that day, four women – two of them Gentile foreigners – were named in the genealogy of Jesus in Matthew's Gospel chapter one.

It is significant that Jesus included women in his teaching, putting them on an equal par with men. The same ethical and moral standards were demanded from both sexes and the same way of salvation was offered to both. Throughout the Bible, women filled significant roles – from leadership like Deborah to unique motherhood like Mary. The same has been true of those in the Suffering Church.

It was Corrie ten Boom who reportedly uttered the notable statement: "When God has a task to be done, he calls a man…a difficult task, he calls a woman!" Recently, a pastor in Cuba told me, "Lenin said that without women there would be no revolution. I say that without women there would be no Church!"

In China, the large group of female Christians who have had a major leadership role in the significant revival and Church growth are rarely referred to locally as 'Pastor' or 'Evangelist' but most often as 'Bible Women'.

This term originated back in the foreign missionary era of the nineteenth century, due to the responsiveness to the Gospel – and then more workers – among females (at least 60 per cent) than males. After the Communist era under Mao Tze-tung began in late 1949 – internally referred to as 'liberation' – significant numbers of pastors were imprisoned on charges of being 'counter-revolutionaries'. In many cases, this left female leadership to care

4

for the flock, especially among the now quickly growing phenomenon of house churches.

During the blackest period of this century's history of China, the Cultural Revolution, Christian women in leadership suffered severely for their faith as well as the male leadership. But from the ashes of this purifying fire has grown a Church that models for the world the reality and power of our risen Saviour.

It is no exaggeration to state that without the witness of women, the Church in China would have died during these terrible years. Today such elderly women are still an inspiration. Chairman Mao often said about China, "Women hold up half the sky." Now it is estimated that about 70 per cent of the active Christian workers in China today are women.

Chinese Bible Woman, Ding Xianggao, is an incredible example. She is a very young itinerant evangelist in China. Very much aware of the cost, she says, "In my country there are many brothers and sisters who suffer for Christ. Some of my co-workers have spent 30 years in prison for the sake of the Gospel." Two of her associates were actually martyred. Because she is a hunted woman, she often sleeps in caves and fields to avoid capture. Her commitment is expressed this way: "Jesus died for me. The least I should do is die for him. To suffer and go to prison for him is my honour, and I look forward to it."

She ended up in a large prison with over 800 inmates involved in prostitution, murder and kidnapping. But Ding believed God had placed her there for a reason. After three years she was released from prison. But not before 78 people had made a commitment to Christ!

Women in leadership has not been a major issue in China's fast-growing Church. 'Great Bible Women of China' introduces you to five of the many, many thousands of Chinese Bible Women. Five that I have had the joy of interviewing and coming to know as a friend. This group is now elderly and have had long fruitful lives of service, yet they continue on unabated. They remind me of the description in Psalm 92: 12-15:

The righteous will flourish like a palm tree,
they will grow like a cedar of Lebanon;

planted in the house of the Lord,
they will flourish in the courts of our God.
They will still bear fruit in old age,
they will stay fresh and green,
proclaiming, "The Lord is upright;
he is my Rock, and there is no wickedness in him."

Because they are involved in vibrant ministry, even today as you read, I have given them pseudonyms. But be assured that they are real people and each incident in their challenging life story is true as they have told it to me. Interspersed among these stories are practical prayer points for Chinese Christian women.

I trust that these short accounts will not only reveal the sensitive spirits and intuitive natures that Christian women of China bring to the task, but also their spiritual maturity in following God's leading and persevering through great trials. My prayer is that after reading this little volume, you – whether male or female – will be challenged to walk more closely with Jesus, and step out in some significant way to serve him and his Suffering Church in China and around the world.

Paul Estabrooks   Toronto, Canada
Minister-at-large   December, 1997
Open Doors International

Sister Alice

The faithful one

"Praise be to the Lord...who daily bears our burdens."
(Psalm 68:19)

The temperature was well below freezing. Beads of perspiration rolled down her body under the multi-layers of winter clothing. Alice grimaced as she continued to push the antiquated Chinese wagon on bicycle wheels. Her strength was nearly depleted. And she shuddered to think of the challenge ahead once she reached her destination in about half an hour.

The axle groaned with complaint as the bent wheels slowly revolved over the frozen mud. She was sure this was the heaviest load of construction rubble she had ever transferred.

"How am I going to lift this heavy load over that perimeter wall? Lord, please help me – again – to get through this day," she silently prayed.

As she plodded on, she reviewed the previous days when she staggered home too exhausted to even eat. Especially that day when she had to shovel cement over her head to the second floor of a new building. All this hard work for only 80 cents a day. This was the accepted lot of a 'counter-revolutionary' in 'liberated' China. Her six children and mother-in-law were now totally dependent on her. Yet an almost imperceptible smile crept to the corners of her mouth.

"How like the Lord to answer my prayer in some unusual way, just like he did so miraculously this morning!"

Alice quickly wiped the perspiration trails from her soft oval face. The salty drops had caused her eyes to sting. Everyone said her large round eyes were her most attractive feature. But now they were causing her pain.

Early ministry

The smile returned as she reminisced how much and how often God had blessed her. Her mind went back to 1936 when as a young Christian and still a teenager she had first met Allen. That changed her life. He was a Bible school student in her home town. Whenever they spent time alone, she recalled how Allen always talked about the ministry to which he felt the Lord calling him. How she loved his sense of calling and commitment. She felt the same way. And Allen knew it. In 1938 they were married and began a ministry of living by faith. They never turned back.

For a moment the tears began to fall as she thought of Allen's past year away from her. Where was he being held captive? Was he still alive? Was he still rejoicing in his Lord? Would she ever see him again?

Her heart leaped at the fond memories of early ministry in the rural provinces – especially those years during the Japanese occupation. They saw hundreds of Chinese people come to Jesus. And in that era, she began to bear their six wonderful children. With the railway lines destroyed by the Japanese war, they returned to the big city and began a local indigenous church ministry there. They were active in street preaching and even radio ministry. Again they saw dozens turn to Christ and discipled every year. And God continued to provide for their every need, even with Allen's mother now living in their home with them and their first three children.

But then came dark memories – the infamous Communist 'liberation'! Nothing was the same from that time onward. Only meetings inside the church buildings were allowed at first. There were years of political wrangling about the newly formed government-approved Church – the Three-Self Patriotic Movement. It was organised to eliminate 'foreign imperialism' from the churches. Allen linked up with the few other key pastors like Watchman Nee and Wang Ming-dao in refusing to join for biblical and spiritual reasons.

Now the tears flowed freely down her icy face as she relived her deepest distress. For the moment she forgot the other aches and pains in her fatigued body. But she would never forget those policemen dragging away her Allen last year. They had told her so roughly she would never see him again. He was to serve a life sentence for being a 'counter-revolutionary' and she was to report to the local Public Security Bureau for 'struggle' meetings on the same charge.

But worst of all was the sadness in the reaction of the children. The older teenagers became quiet and withdrawn. Little six-year-old Mei Lin cried every night calling for "baba".

"Lord, be with Allen today, and let him know I love him and miss him so. Keep him safe wherever he is. And keep him in the centre of your loving, protecting hand!"

Alice wanted to block the next memories because they were so hurtful. She briefly skimmed over the daily six-hour struggle sessions when she was tortured with repeated shouts to renounce her religious beliefs and divorce Allen. "If I did not know the Lord, I would commit suicide," she thought to herself. Her acute memory instantly recollected the two other women she knew who recently went insane and did commit suicide under similar circumstances.

She hung on with the help of God. Her strategy earlier this morning was the same as other days. She closed her eyes and prayed to endure the struggle sessions. Utterly exhausted, she left those lengthy meetings to begin her eight-hour heavy manual labour shift. "Without the help of Allen's mother looking after the children, I'd never be able to cope," she mused.

God's encouragement

A slight smile returned as she thought of their recent experiences. "Mother worries so much!" Just yesterday Mother had come to Alice on her arrival home from work: "There's no more rice left after dinner tonight. I've used it all up! Tomorrow I'll go and visit my daughter early and see if I can borrow some for breakfast."

Alice shivered as she recalled her own fear. This is what she had always been so concerned about with Allen's arrest and imprisonment. And now the day had arrived. There was no more rice for the children. They had lived through many days already with neither vegetables nor meat. And even worse was the fact she had no money to buy anything. Now Mother was going to have to go and beg from other family members.

How angry she remembered feeling at that moment. "God, you promised to take care of me and my family, and now there is no more food!" she had chided the Lord. Her keen memory quickly flashed onward to her evening Bible reading. How incredible that the Bible fell open to Matthew chapter six. Her eyes fell on verse 26: *"Look at the birds of the air; they do not sow or reap or store away in barns, and yet your heavenly Father feeds them. Are you not much more valuable than they?"*

Oh, how convicted Alice had felt at reading those words! She fell on her knees and with many tears of repentance begged God to forgive her. She then thanked him that he would indeed be her provider and fell asleep peacefully.

The wheels began moving faster as Alice quickened her pace. The warm memories seemed to pump adrenalin into her exhausted body. They flooded back into her mind, almost overwhelming her. For a moment she forgot about the cold and pain. She so relished reliving the events of early this morning...

As she was washing, there was a knock at the door. It was only five minutes to six. Some of the children's friends came by early – but not this early! She threw on her Chinese housecoat, stoked the charcoal fire in their little metal stove in the centre of the room and put the water kettle on to heat for tea. When she opened the door, a fiercely cold wind blew on her face. But her heart was strangely warmed as she stared into the friendly but anxious face of an elderly lady holding a big box. Alice had never seen her before.

"Are you Sister Alice?" she queried with some agitation. "Oh good, I've had a very difficult time finding you!" And with those words she quickly shuffled into the house, setting the big box on the kitchen table. Alice closed the door to keep out the chilling wind and cold. The elderly lady moved to the stove, warming her hands above the winter fire. She had an extremely peaceful glow in her eyes. Yet she seemed uncomfortable in the house. She started for the door to leave.

"Wait a minute! What's your name? Won't you stay for some

hot tea?" Alice had quickly blurted out.

The lady hesitated and then responded, "I have no name. Just thank the Lord for that box!" She walked out the door and disappeared as quickly as she had come.

Alice was stunned. With trembling hands she opened the box. By now Mother and all the children, eager with anticipation, were around the table as well. There was a large bag of rice, some meat and vegetables, and at the very bottom of the box an envelope. In the envelope was 50 dollars! She fell into one of the kitchen chairs and began to weep. Fifty dollars was a lot of money for a common labourer who earned 80 cents a day. God was so good!

"Thank you Lord. Are you also caring for my Allen the same way in his prison experience?"

Temptation

One wheel fell into a frozen rut. The wagon lurched and then came to a sudden halt. Alice pushed with all her strength but nothing moved. She was now at the very end of her energy but still had one block further to go. And then that perimeter wall to cross! Suddenly two strong arms grabbed the pushing bar and the wagon slowly, complainingly moved ahead again.

"Cheng Ho! What a surprise to see you here!"

"I have the papers ready for you to sign, Alice," Cheng Ho softly intoned straining to keep the wagon rolling.

"What papers?"

"Your divorce papers, of course!"

"What more challenges will I have to face today, Lord?" Alice quickly thought.

"Cheng Ho, I've told you repeatedly that I am a Christian. I cannot divorce or remarry!"

Cheng Ho responded with a sardonic smile. "But Alice, you know the Public Security Bureau chief will not leave you alone until you comply with his wishes. Marry me and they will erase your bad records and make them like new. You won't have to carry any more heavy burdens. And they'll even give us a new house for your family to live in. You really have no other choice!"

They reached the perimeter wall. Cheng Ho enlisted the help of a friend passing by and the wagon was quickly over the wall and at its destination. "Thank you Lord for answering my prayer about the wall. And please help me to answer Cheng Ho with your love," Alice prayed.

She thought of the many gifts of clothing and money he had repeatedly offered her. And then that quiet knock on the door at midnight a week ago asking to come share her bed for the night! Alice was flattered with the attention, yet pleaded with the Lord to give her strength to do what was right. With a warm smile in her large round eyes, she responded, "Cheng Ho. You are a good man. And I am thankful for your concern and help (especially just now with the wagon!). But as long as I know my Allen is alive, I can't even think of living with another man."

"And how do you know he's alive? Anyway, he's been given a life sentence. No counter-revolutionary has ever returned home," Cheng Ho rebutted.

"The Lord daily assures me Allen is alive and well. And I'm trusting God to bring him back to me," she gently replied. Dejectedly, Cheng Ho trudged off home.

Alice too began the long trek home, now ignoring the cold. "I wonder what Mother has prepared for dinner from the new food box that arrived this morning? Lord, you are so good! Please be good to my Allen today too!"

The answer to prayer

After serving 21 years and eight months of his life sentence, Allen was miraculously released and returned to the loving arms of faithful Alice...and to their six now grown-up children.

For the next ten years he was on probation with no freedom to travel. During this time, Alice's ministry changed again. Their home was always full of visitors and Christian friends. Allen preached, taught and counselled while Alice ministered hospitality. They started evening Bible studies together and later a house fellowship. Today it is the largest house church in their city.

At the time of writing, Alice is 79 years young. She concludes,

"Twenty-one years and eight months of separation is a long time. But God led us through. Today we have ten grandchildren. All but one of our children are walking with the Lord. Looking back, I think hardships are good for children and families because God is faithful."

God is faithful. And so is his child, Alice.

"God sets the lonely in families, he leads forth the prisoners with singing." (Psalm 68:6a)

Practical prayer point: training

"I have more than 1,000 young people who are willing to dedicate their lives to serve the Lord," said Wen Jou, a Chinese house church leader who recently attended an Open Doors training seminar in central China. "Yet they hardly know anything. They need training.

"This is the reason that I have come here – so that I can learn and then train those eager young people," she added. Getting to the training session was no easy task for Wen Jou, who had to journey ten hours in an antiquated bus and another 50 hours by train.

In her mid-50s, Wen has a very limited education and yet shoulders an enormous responsibility. She was converted through her own miraculous healing. The coffin that had been prepared for her burial became her pulpit. As she preached, people came from all over China to hear her story and receive Christ.

"We now have 1,000 meeting points throughout the region, established by God's miraculous work," she adds. "But we lack leaders among us who have enough knowledge to lead us to maturity in our faith!"

Please pray for the many women leaders with little training themselves and many followers who are in great need of the same.

Aunty Esther

The fool for Christ

"Do not deceive yourselves. If any one of you thinks he is wise by the standards of this age, he should become a 'fool' so that he may become wise." (1 Corinthians 3:18)

Diminutive Aunty Esther warmly welcomed Nora to her small Chinese home with a large smile and "Praise the Lord!" Her dark glasses framed a friendly, well-weathered face. Esther was especially excited to see the big bag of Bibles since her supply had recently been depleted.

"Please excuse me for a few moments," she said to Nora, "because I'm discipling a young lady who just received the Lord a few days ago. She works for the *Daily News* and has no Bible. Now I can give her one of these you brought."

Nora was happy to wait. Then she spent time in prayer and fellowship with this elderly Chinese saint who has a perpetual overflow of joy. Aunty Esther shared how her supply of Bibles was quickly exhausted because of the great demand for God's Word. There were always new Christians on her waiting list.

Since the next day was Sunday, Nora asked for directions to the Three Self Protestant church in the city where she could observe a Chinese worship service. Nora's Chinese companion went with her to interpret what turned out to be a very evangelistic and biblically sound message. After the sermon, three people went to the front altar to pray.

As Nora and her companion were about to leave, a group of young Australian tourists approached them with a problem. "We heard that Bibles were badly needed here in China," they started, "so we went to the Bible Society in Australia and bought a bagful. But when we came to this church today, one of the pastors told us they don't need any more Bibles here. They now print their own. And they wouldn't accept our gift! Do you know what we can do with them?"

"I gladly relieved them from their quandary," Nora beamed as she reported later, "and put the bag on my shoulder to leave. But just then the three people who had been praying at the front were coming back up the aisle. And to my surprise one was Aunty Esther and another was the new believer she had been discipling the day before."

Aunty Esther ran to Nora and excitedly shared that the third person was the young lady's fiancé who had just prayed the sinner's prayer at the altar and committed his life to Jesus. Then her smiling face turned solemn. "But I've already distributed all the Bibles you brought yesterday. I've none left for this young man."

Nora placed Esther's hand on the bulging shoulder bag. "God has provided – again!"

Miracle child

Nora spent as much time as possible at Aunty Esther's home. She says, "I sense God's presence in this room." It is tiny by western standards – about 12 by 20 feet. It contains her bed with a steel framework around it and a platform on top which holds the treasures of a lifetime: a desk with a well loved Bible laying open on it, two worn chairs, a little round table, a small potbellied stove, and an old piano. The walls are covered with photographs, posters and calligraphy banners with favourite Scriptures on them.

They sip Chinese tea from blue-lidded cups and Nora requests this dynamic little lady to share about her life. She smiles and looks briefly into the distance. Leaning forward in her chair she begins her story...

Esther was born on Christmas Day in 1909, in a cold, northern province of China. At the age of 40 days she was found, cold and blue in her bed, hardly breathing because of pneumonia. She was taken to an English doctor who happened to be Hudson Taylor's son. The doctor prayed over the baby and told the mother to keep her in a basin of warm water, to pray continuously and trust God that she would be revived. For many hours it looked as if their labours were in vain. But on the third day, the mother detected the baby's breath and within a short time, her daughter's colour returned and she was breathing normally.

The often repeated story of her recovery left a deep impression on young Esther. At a very young age, she sensed God's call on her life to preach his Word in interior China; and she made a decision to be a paediatrician, like Dr. Taylor.

She studied hard and was always first in her class. In her early 20s she completed her degree in medicine at a Chinese extension school of New York State University. Then she became ill with typhoid fever. Near to death, she was placed in quarantine in a back room of the hospital. Every day she grew weaker and it appeared she would not recover. But God had other plans. One night a nurse came in to check on her and she asked if there was anything she wanted.

"A Bible," she whispered.

For the next seven days, Esther read the Bible through as God clearly showed her his plan of salvation. In that dark little hospital room where she had been placed to die, Esther began to live again as she asked Jesus to be the Lord of her life. And the fever broke. The next year, she was married to a wonderful Christian man. That was in late June 1937. Years went by with Esther doctoring and her husband preaching.

Medical missionary

There was one more message the Lord had for his daughter. He gently reminded her one day, "What are you doing in this city when I called you to preach the Gospel in interior China?"

In obedience to God, Esther spent many fruitful years in missionary service with her preacher-husband in south-western China. One of her favourite memories of the time relates to a vice-president of the university. He was very sick and after seeing many other doctors came to her for advice.

"I'm very sorry! As a doctor there are many diseases I cannot treat," Esther told him. "But I will introduce you to the greatest physician I know." She gave him a Gospel tract.

One night soon after this, he came to visit her. He shared that as a young student in London, he had often attended church. After studying law, he returned to China and joined the Communist Party. He forgot about the Lord and now was suffering and empty.

"Your father in Heaven is calling you to come home tonight," Esther responded. And she began singing the hymn, "Softly and tenderly Jesus is calling…come home." Moved with emotion, the university vice-president knelt on the floor and prayed to the Lord for forgiveness. He was coming home.

Esther says, "I didn't pray for him to be healed but at his next check-up he was completely better."

The fool for christ

Then came the dreaded Cultural Revolution in the mid-60s. She was in charge of eight paediatric wards at a large hospital back in her home city. The Communists were beginning to crack down on people who did not toe the party line, worked for a foreign company, or had any form of advanced education.

Early one morning, Esther was rudely awakened by four nurses who pulled her from her bed and marched her on foot to the hospital. She was to be 'invited' to join the party which would require her to renounce her faith in Jesus.

On the way there, the nurses stopped at a hairdresser and shaved off half of Esther's hair. Then, confronted by the Communist leaders, she said she would consider their invitation if she could continue to practice her faith in Jesus Christ. At the mention of his Name, she was thrown down and cursed. Very soon after, while doing her rounds in the hospital one morning, a Communist official came to her, tore the stethoscope from her neck and said, "You are no longer Esther; now you are The Fool."

For the next 11 years this tiny, gracious little lady lived in the basement of the hospital and obediently submitted to her new job, to clean the toilets and reception area floors of the wards of which she was once the head. Her meagre salary of 50 yuan a month was reduced to 15 yuan (then equal to a dollar). It went first to buy the cleaning materials, then for food.

But Esther did her tasks with joy in her heart for she had found true meaning in a personal relationship with Christ. His presence was with her and she sang as she worked. Those who oversaw her work marvelled at her attitude, and secretly envied her joy. Like the apostle Paul, she was a fool for Christ.

How do saints of God endure this persecution for so long? Esther says, "We spiritualised everything. The cleaning water represented the Holy Spirit. The cleaning rag represented the Word of God. The toilets were peoples' hearts before God touched them. I cleaned the latrines thoroughly applying the Word of God and the Holy Spirit to their hearts.

She says with a twinkle in her eye, "My hospital had the cleanest toilets and floors in all of China because we wanted the cleanest hearts in all of China. People would ask me, 'How can you be so joyful, so happy doing such a menial job when you should be in charge of this hospital?'

"I would respond, 'It doesn't matter what job you have or what your position, it only matters that you love Jesus and are faithful and loyal to him.'"

In 1977, she felt a hand on her shoulder one day as she was scrubbing the floor. "Esther," he said. Oh, how long it had been since she had been called by her real name! "You can go home now. You will receive your pension as a concession of Chairman Mao." Esther didn't question him even though she knew Mao had died the year before.

So home she went to the dwelling which has been home to her family off and on since 1936. And in a gesture that can only be called a miracle, she was awarded full back pay for the years she had lost from her profession, an amount equivalent to $13,000! This money was to sustain her family and helped to educate her children.

Hospital evangelism

Aunty Esther pauses to refill the hot water pot for tea and then continues to share. She tells of the miracles that surrounded the time of her husband's death. He was very ill at home and Esther

18

felt he was dying. His faith was extremely strong. When he came upon Exodus 15:26, *"I am the Lord, who heals you,"* he felt the Lord do a mighty work in his body. Together they thanked God for this miracle of healing.

Their daughter, Mary, who was not yet a believer, came home with an ambulance to take her father to the hospital. Strangely, neither Esther nor her husband protested, as they both felt God was directing them to go to hospital even though he had received healing. He was placed in a ward with five critically ill patients who each had several family members with them.

The Lord spoke to Esther, "Preach my Word," and Esther began to tell everyone in that hospital room about God's plan of salvation. Fifteen patients and relatives placed their trust in Jesus Christ that day. The next day one of the patients was totally healed. He had been a Party member.

Aunty Esther's husband was in the hospital for 31 days, and every few days he would be moved to a different ward to be checked by different doctors and she would start at the beginning, winning more souls to the Lord.

One day he whispered to her, "I'm going home today." She knew in her spirit he meant home to his beloved Father in Heaven and she called the family to come and say farewell. All that long night Esther held his hand and felt his pulse slow down, and finally stop. In the morning the doctor confirmed he was dead. An extensive autopsy was done but the cause of his death was never medically identified.

Daughter Mary grieved for her father and when she returned from the funeral, she sat at the piano he so loved to play. As she placed her fingers on the old keys, talent not unlike her father's began to express itself in her playing. She asked her mother if the spirit of a dead loved one could be transferred to another. Her mother put her arms around her and told her that only the Holy Spirit of God could have gifted her with this. In that moment, Mary gave her life to Christ and asked him to come and live in her heart.

No time to retire

Those 11 years as Christ's 'Fool' and her month of joyously sharing the Good News of salvation in the critical care wards were not wasted. Some hospitals later continued to invite Aunty Esther to return three times a year to share the Word of God with doctors, nurses and patients. Every Saturday she participated in a day of prayer and fasting with many other medical workers who also followed the Lord.

But Esther's favourite witnessing method is bus evangelism. She boards a local city bus at its terminus where she is sure to get a seat. During its run, with people crowded like sardines inside, Aunty Esther reads aloud stories about Jesus from her Bible. If anyone shows interest, she hands them a slip of paper with her address and an invitation to come to her home and talk. She does not fear the authorities, who treat this kind of activity with severity. She is often quoted as saying, "At my age and after all I've suffered, what can they do to me now?" Her strategies for personal evangelism helped her lead dozens of people to Jesus, including some very high placed people in the Chinese government and media circles. She is also prepared for the discipling that follows.

On one occasion she led to the Lord and discipled a young lady who worked for the government news service. At a staff Christmas party, this young lady sang a Christmas carol about the birth of Jesus. She subsequently lost her job. Esther says, "It costs to follow Jesus here in China."

A total Bible Woman

Because of her active evangelism and discipling, it was not long before Aunty Esther was seeking out assistance for the many Bibles she needed. She had a wooden box built under her bed and requested Open Doors workers, "Please don't let my box go empty!" Dozens of couriers have trekked to her door over the years to keep the box full.

Esther told the Lord that she would witness to anyone whom he sent to her door. One day a policeman came by to check why so many foreigners were visiting. At first Esther's heart began pounding with fear. But she remembered her promise to the Lord, invited the policeman in for tea and shared the Gospel with him.

Aunty Esther smiles wistfully as she remembers repeated occasions of God's faithfulness. She loves to sing and pray. Her singing is spontaneous. Six to eight times a day she intercedes in extended prayer. The bottom line of Aunty Esther's years of service is this: minister faithfully to anyone as God gives opportunity. And even when persecuted be happy in the Lord.

"Those who are wise will shine like the brightness of the heavens, and those who lead many to righteousness, like the stars forever and ever."   (Daniel 12:3)

Practical prayer point: Bibles

"Every week we come across believers in villages who have no Bibles," said a house church leader recently. "Just last week we found an entire community of 400 believers who didn't actually know there was such a thing as a Bible. They had been living off the words of a hymn book, and presumed that Jesus' teachings had been lost. How excited they were to have his words!"

An Open Doors contact in central China had this to say: "When we first received the Bibles and literature from you, most of us cried. We realised that the brothers and sisters overseas have not forgotten us and we feel so thankful. Because there is still not enough Christian resource material to meet our needs, we can only give them to the leaders of the cell groups. When one of our members receives a book, there is sometimes a temptation not to share it with others because it is so precious and rare. If we can have more Bibles and Christian study books, we'll have plenty to share with everyone."

There are literally millions of Christians living in rural China who don't have a copy of the Bible – let alone any other Christian books. Please pray for the Open Doors co-workers who are involved in programmes of literature distribution. Ask God to blind the eyes of the authorities to enable Bibles and Christian books to get into the hands of hungry believers.

Aunty Mary

The fearless witness

"Now get up and stand on your feet. I have appeared to you to appoint you as a servant and as a witness of what you have seen of me and what I will show you." (Acts 26:16)

She muttered to herself as she stomped down the road. Her hurried steps were more impatient than usual. The pavement shopkeepers and food-servers noticed her pace and thought she was angry or worried. But the faint smile on Mary's face belied her body language. The only thing different about this trip down her dusty city street was the 'Jesus' video in her hand. She held it close to herself like a treasure chest.

"Lord, please let my plan work," she telegraphed.

The bright sunshine made her greying hair seem whiter than usual.

Mary's blood was still boiling from the Public Security Bureau raid on her home earlier that day. A large group of police officers had suddenly swarmed her small apartment. Easily finding her sizeable store of Bibles and other Christian literature, they roughly impounded them and carried everything away to their own store. They then warned her not to accept any more Bibles that were brought in unofficially from abroad.

"We will always be watching," they taunted her.

"Lord, why did you let this happen?" Mary had earlier queried. But then a strange peace had settled over her agitated spirit. And her eyes fell on the 'Jesus' video still resting on the top of the bookcase.

She turned the corner to the left when she reached the main street. She could now see her destination two long blocks down this wide tree-lined avenue. Mary began to rehearse again what she would say on arrival.

"Lord, please help me to keep a positive attitude," she prayed again. The young lady at the desk looked askance in her direction.

"I want to talk to the Chief of Police!" Mary demanded firmly. Mary's soft face and gentle spirit appealed to the receptionist. But she put up her normal false front.

"He's very busy right now. Do you have an appointment?"

"No. But today his men were at my house and they did not see this," she said waving the video tape in the air.

The receptionist was nonplussed. Why would this lady volunteer such information? As though in obedience to a master, she ushered Mary into the police chief's office. He pretended to be oblivious to her arrival yet grunted a question of intent.

"Sir," Mary began slowly, "earlier today your men raided my house and took all the Bibles I had stored there. I understand that they were just doing their job. But after they left, I noticed that they missed this video tape. I need to know from you if this is acceptable material or not. Would you and your staff check it for me?"

At first the chief's response was disgust. Yet the sincerity in her voice and on her face prodded him to give it a second thought. "Very well, come back in two weeks," he muttered dismissing her with a wave of the hand.

Mary almost skipped out the door with overflowing joy as she headed toward home. "Thank you Lord! How else could I get the chief of police with his staff to watch 'Jesus'?"

Directed steps

As she now strolled towards home, she recounted how God had given her opportunities to witness all her long life. From the time of her conversion as a young woman and subsequent friendship with Watchman Nee's wife, she had turned down study and career advancement opportunities to be a missionary in interior China. She made sure she visited all her university classmates to share the Gospel with them. They were now successful medical doctors.

Mary smiled as she remembered just how successful her own missionary work had been during the Japanese occupation and the war years that followed. So much so that she had given up her medical career.

"Lord, you do all things well!" she whispered. "And thanks to you, I haven't had one day of sickness in my 80 plus years."

Suddenly a transient thought raced through her active memory. She immediately spun her body to the left and headed west. "Oh, I promised Pastor that I would join him for dinner with some foreign guests tonight," she mused. "I almost forgot! But I must be home by nine to hear my favourite program on FEBC radio!"

She spotted them as soon as she entered the hotel dining room. Pastor was busy sharing his long testimony of God's faithfulness as she approached the round table. The conversation halted as introductions were made all around and she gracefully took her place. She quickly shared her mixed emotions with Pastor and the group about what had happened to her that day.

"The Lord is making the situation here such that you have to depend on the Holy Spirit. Please pray for the chief of police. Pray that he and his staff will watch the video and want to know and follow Jesus!" she concluded.

Living testimony

"Where did you learn such good English, Mary?" the group leader asked.

"I went to a Methodist girl's school run by missionaries many years ago."

Pastor then continued his story of long term imprisonment before, during, and after the Cultural Revolution.

"And what happened to you during this time, Mary?" the leader asked again. Mary hesitated. She did not even want to relive the horrible memories. But she knew it would encourage the group to hear another testimony of God's faithfulness in helping her persevere.

"My problems really started with 'liberation'," she began. "My large family property and home that I inherited was confiscated and I was assigned a small flat. Because I spent all my time in Christian witness and ministry, I was forced into a 'mental' hospital for psychological treatment. Maybe it was also because I refused to become a Communist. They tried everything on me and finally gave up. I was released. Praise the Lord!

"During the Cultural Revolution, all church meetings and home fellowships were closed. All Bibles and hymn books were confiscated. Anyone with an education received extra harsh treatment. Because I was trained as a medical doctor, I was forced to work as a street sweeper like other educated people.

"Because I was known for the fellowship held in my home, the Red Guards came and took away my personal Bible. They treated me very badly and then stuck large posters on my door saying, 'She preaches the Gospel. She is a counter-revolutionary!' Every day I was subjected to repeated 'criticism' meetings and forced to study the political thought of Mao Tze-tung. It hurts to even think about that time. I was supposed to save my 'soul' through reforming my way of thinking.

"It always impressed me that in his writings Mao, though himself a Communist, often referred to the saving of a person's 'soul'. During the Cultural Revolution, 'soul' was mentioned frequently. In speeches made from Tiananmen Square, the Red Guards were often encouraged to allow the revolutionary spirit to touch their 'souls' in order to improve themselves. The Cultural Revolution touched the 'soul' of every person. But the Christian has a secret place with the Lord that no one can touch!"

Mary concluded, "What I can say about my Christian walk with Jesus is simply this: love the Lord more than anyone or anything! The government Church asks you to love your country above all else. We Chinese believers have paid a price to follow Jesus. But we can still pay much more."

The group of visitors had been quickly taking notes. Now they just looked at each other and shook their heads as though in disbelief.

Ministry in the mountains

Mary's quick question snapped them out of this response. "Has any of you been to Lhasa, Tibet?"

They all shook their heads.

"Oh, the Lord has put this group of unreached people on my heart," she continued. "They are such spiritually needy people. Tibet is the darkest spot in the world. But God is building his Church even in Tibet. I'm going back there next month on another mission trip. Please pray for me. Last time I fainted from the thin air up there. And my nose bled frequently. But I'm committed to go there and shine for Jesus.

"At the fellowship of believers in the capital, I taught them to sing, 'He is Lord' and 'I Have Decided To Follow Jesus, No Turning Back'. We need to reach more people for Jesus. He is saying, 'You need to hurry and get the job done so I can come back again!' But the only way to win them is one by one."

Her excitement made her sentences seem disjointed. By now the group leader could not contain himself. "Don't you Chinese Christians ever retire?" he blurted out.

Pastor, an octogenarian, interrupted. "Retire! Where do you read about that in the Bible?" Again the group shook their heads, this time with a loud chuckle.

"No," Pastor continued, "Jesus said, 'Work while it is yet day for the night is coming when no man can work!'"

Mary interjected, "I need to get home now. I'm expecting another visitor tonight. A young lady from Inner Mongolia is coming for a discipleship class. She just received Jesus last week. But before I go, please let me leave some prayer requests with you. Please pray for the many lost souls here in China. Pray for the many Bibles and training materials needed by the fast-growing Church here. And also pray that more Sauls will be turned into Pauls! I'm referring to government leaders coming to know Jesus."

Mary said her farewells and was prepared to walk home. But the group would hear nothing of it. They ultimately prevailed on her to at least let them hire a taxi to take her home.

The joy of giving

She knew something was different as soon as she walked into her flat.

"Hi, Aunty Mary," said Gary bounding around the corner in his colourful sarong. "I let myself in – as usual. There is a young lady here waiting for you too. I couldn't understand her accented Mandarin."

"Gary," responded Mary with a hug, "I didn't expect you until tomorrow! What happened?"

"I thought I'd surprise you since I got home a day early from Vietnam!"

"The taxi driver just prayed outside to receive the Lord!" she joyfully exploded, changing the subject. "He had been listening to Christian radio broadcasts and I simply encouraged him to pray the sinner's prayer – and he did!"

"Praise the Lord! And who is this young lady waiting here?"

"Oh, she's a new believer. Came to our city all the way from Inner Mongolia. She really needs the fullness of the Holy Spirit. Let me spend an hour with her and then we'll have some tea. I want to hear all about your trip to Vietnam! By the way, take any Bibles you brought for me over to Pastor's place right away. Be careful. They're watching! Everything I had here was confiscated today."

Mary had already forgotten about her favourite Christian radio broadcast now being aired from FEBC Manila as she began the discipleship lesson. Before long she and Gary – a tall, blonde New Zealander – were deep in conversation. Even though it was officially discouraged, Gary loved to stay at Mary's flat on his short visits to China. She was such an inspiration.

He shared at length the exciting growth of believers in Vietnam as well as the shortage of Bibles and spiritual books and training materials.

"Sounds like here in China!" she softly interjected. Mary sat in rapt attention as Gary explained how new believers in one house church network memorise Psalm 119 in order to get on the list of those approved to receive a Bible when they are available.

"Oh Gary!" she responded with deep emotion. "Those believers in Vietnam need to have God's Word." She began to fumble with the money belt at her waist and pulled out 300 yuan. "This is all the money I have, Gary. But I want you to take it and buy Bibles for those new believers in Vietnam!"

Though a simple lady living a simple lifestyle, Aunty Mary is a testimony of God's goodness over a long, joyful lifetime. Now in her early 90s, she continues to be a fearless witness for Jesus.

"You sympathised with those in prison and joyfully accepted the confiscation of your property, because you knew that you yourselves had better and lasting possessions. So do not throw away your confidence; it will be richly rewarded. You need to persevere so that when you have done the will of God, you will receive what he has promised."

(Hebrews 10:34-36)

Practical prayer point: Loneliness

Please pray for the spouses (and children) of house church leaders, especially in-country trainers that conduct our seminars. Some of them are gone from home for six months at a time. The wife of one of the leaders found herself alone for half a year, as no one dared to visit her for security reasons. But she was left with no source of income, and no fellowship.

One day an elderly sister knocked on her door with two large sacks of instant noodles. The older sister said, "I'm too old to bother about getting arrested; I just had to be with her." The wife responded, "I felt like Elijah being fed by the ravens...at my darkest hour God provided." Pray for all those who find loneliness the price they pay for following Jesus.

Sister Lucy

The freedom lover

"I know your deeds. See, I have placed before you an open door that no one can shut. I know that you have little strength, yet you have kept my word and have not denied my name." (Revelations 3:8)

Her fingers ached from overwork. And her large frame heaved a sigh of exhaustion. She knew it was late – or early morning – as the lantern light was growing very dim. Though physically tired, in spirit she was exhilarated at the number of copies of *'Streams In The Desert'* she had now completely copied by hand.

Lucy yawned and reached for her glass of hot tea. In a few hours she would be back in the rice fields doing the back-breaking harvesting work until darkness fell again. This prisoner lifestyle had been hers for so long she could hardly remember anything else. But she still had dreams and hopes!

"Lord, if you ever allow me to live in freedom at home again, I want to be involved in literature production and distribution among your family," she silently prayed.

"Live in freedom…live in freedom," she mused. "What would it be like?"

This was her ninth year of living in exile, consigned to a hard labour farm during the infamous Cultural Revolution era. Before this she had spent 15 years in China's notorious prisons. As she sipped her tea, she noted how the veins stood out on the back of her aching hands. She glanced in the mirror and scrutinised the wrinkles on her round, soft face and the streaks of grey in her black hair pulled into a bun at the back hiding most of her large ears. How the years take their toll!

Soon her thoughts turned to the future again. Her spirit burst out into song. This was not unusual for Lucy, as music lifted her spirits and gave her renewed hope:

Jesus, Saviour, pilot me
Over life's tempestuous sea;
Unknown waves before me roll,
Hiding rocks and treacherous shoal;
Chart and compass came from Thee:
Jesus, Saviour, pilot me.

Early life

The song was fresh in her mind because only days earlier she had met another Christian worker. It was so cold and they were so wet from the rain, they had to hug each other for warmth. In that situation they sang together, 'Jesus Saviour Pilot Me'.

She had not always believed the words of that song even though she knew them from childhood. She thought back to those years when her Christian mother and pastor father failed in trying to control her young, rebellious will. After school she had married Li An and involved herself deeply in business but there was no room for the Lord in her life.

Soon came a daughter, Mei Lee, and the devastation of learning that Li An was having an affair. Life became meaningless when he left her and went to Taiwan. Her mother pleaded with her to attend a local church and she lied that she was doing so. Instead, she frequented dance halls and lost herself in drink.

All she had left was the business. She threw herself into making money through the mechanised rice processing plant. Although the Communists had brought 'liberation' to China, in her small community she was somehow allowed to continue her capitalist ways since she employed a good number of local people. At the height of her wealth, there was a big fire at the plant. She was suspected of arson and was arrested and imprisoned.

During this first imprisonment she became desperate and constantly contemplated suicide. But then the Holy Spirit began his gentle work in her heart. She was often reminded of her early upbringing, especially in songs. She remembered the special meetings of Chinese evangelist Dr. John Sung when she was nine. She had loved to sing the song:

> Come, every soul by sin oppressed,
> There's mercy with the Lord,
> And He will surely give you rest
> By trusting in His word.
> Only trust Him, only trust Him,
> Only trust Him now.
> He will save you, He will save you,
> He will save you now.

There in the prison cell, she tearfully asked God for forgiveness for her wilfulness and sinfulness and gave her heart to him. She also committed her future into his hands. For the first time, a sense of peace flooded her being and she did not resent being in jail. But the imprisonment was to be short. After investigations were completed, she was exonerated and freed. She continued with the business but turned her back on a life of luxury.

Church life

What Lucy did concentrate on was her local church and becoming a true disciple of Jesus Christ. She devoured materials by Watchman Nee that she acquired through Gospel Publishing in Shanghai. She transcribed her pastor's sermons, printed and circulated them. This began her interest and life-long passion for producing Christian literature.

In early January 1956, members of her church congregation were being arrested. There was pressure through 'struggle' sessions being placed on the pastor. Knowing that difficult days lay ahead, the faithful group of believers met secretly for a communion service. She remembered crying as she heard for the first time the song:

> I gave My life for thee,
> My precious blood I shed,
> That thou might'st ransomed be,
> And quickened from the dead;
> I gave, I gave My life for thee,
> What hast thou given for Me?

Even now tears came to her eyes as she remembered that night and that song. How God had used those words through his Spirit all during her imprisonment as a source of encouragement. Days later she and the pastor along with many others were arrested. Through many 'struggle' sessions, she was interrogated and pressured to denounce her pastor. These sessions lasted for two years and eight months.

During this time, she was kept in a prison cell with seven other women. As a result of her music and quiet witness, all seven received the Lord Jesus as their Saviour. To keep her quiet, the authorities put her in solitary confinement as punishment. Another Christian lady was also in a solitary confinement cell. Between the two of them, the authorities placed a demon-possessed man who screamed all night long. No one could sleep.

Lucy prayed for the man in the name of Jesus and God drove the demon out of the man. Once healed, he received the Lord through communications in a small hole in the wall. He carried messages between the two Christian sisters. When the authorities discovered it, they released him.

"Whatever you are suffering, God will bring some positive results," thought Lucy.

She was finally officially sentenced to eight years' imprisonment as a counter-revolutionary. But through it all, she refused to denounce her pastor or tell lies to save her skin.

Prison life was no easier than the years of interrogation. It was to be 're-education' experience as well as punishment. There was tremendous pressure to change people's minds. Some were even beaten to death in the process. To receive daily food – mostly rice – work quotas were required and often increased. Lucy was a rice worker, planting in the spring, hoeing in the summer and carrying heavy loads from the fields to the barn during harvest in the autumn.

At night there were political films to complete the re-education. If you didn't watch them, you were required to carry heavy sandbags and were also given extra physical duties during the day.

The rock

One evening, Lucy was part of a group of ten Christian counter-revolutionaries who were required to move a very large and heavy rock. Some other strong women offered to help them as thanks for the Christian ladies' assistance in writing letters for them. With chains and big sticks they successfully moved the rock. They worked together with such joy and happiness, the prison cadre came out at midnight to see what was going on.

"Since you are so enthusiastic," he bellowed, "now move the rock back to its original place! Without the help of the other women – only you counter-revolutionaries!" Instead, the tired and happy prisoners went to sleep.

The next morning, the prison cadre discovered it was Lucy who suggested this, so he ordered the others to work in the fields and Lucy to move the rock back all alone. She remembered standing on the huge rock, raising her hands and praying, "Lord, you see how they persecute us. Now it's your turn to take action. Your children are suffering here and this miracle will bring glory to you!"

The large rock was wide at the top and narrow at the bottom. A prisoner passed by, and suggested that it was better not to roll the rock on its wide side or it would get stuck. So Lucy used a fulcrum and pried and shoved the rock back to its original place. The prison cadre was amazed. Seeing the marks on the ground, he asked, "Who helped you?"

Lucy answered, "My God helped me!"

The cadre responded, "Look at her. She is so strong and wise she moved the rock all alone. But last night she needed all your help." Many prisoners received the Lord as a result of this miracle of God. The experience brought to Lucy's mind another of her favourite songs:

> Got any rivers you think are uncrossable?
> Got any mountains you can't tunnel through?
> God specialises in things thought impossible,
> He does the things others cannot do.

Even witnessing was made possible by using very creative means. One prisoner spent every free moment scratching scripture verses explaining the Gospel in very small Chinese characters on her cell bed made of rough wooden planks. Years later, she met people who were in the same cell and had come to know and follow the Lord through reading and meditating on those scripture texts.

Because she was not 're-educatable,' Lucy's prison sentence was extended for four years and then another three years. After 15 years of imprisonment, she was exiled to nine years of hard farming work in a remote village in the mountains. In exile, she used every spare minute to hand-copy spiritual messages for the many believers who otherwise had nothing. She sang the second verse:

> As a mother stills her child,
> Thou canst hush the ocean wild;
> Boisterous waves obey Thy will
> When Thou say'st to them, "Be still!"
> Wondrous Sovereign of the sea,
> Jesus, Saviour, pilot me.

After a total of 24 years, Lucy was finally released to return to her home. As she had promised the Lord, her first activity was distributing Scriptures – in the cities and especially to the remote rural areas. She shared a large number of Bibles from 'Project Pearl' – one million Chinese Bibles delivered by Open Doors to coastal China and distributed throughout the land.

Later she developed her own production and distribution network system. She calls it 'The Gospel Machine' and rejoices that it has a significant impact on her region's Bible needs. She lives and works completely by faith. Lucy's life answers the question Jesus asks in her favourite song:

> I gave, I gave My life for thee.
> What hast thou given for Me?

"They overcame him by the blood of the Lamb and by the word of their testimony; they did not love their lives so much as to shrink from death."   (Revelations 12:11)

Practical prayer point: Prison

Pray for China's women leaders who even today find themselves in prison as a result of their bold witness for the Lord. Sister Agnes shares her prison testimony:

"At the beginning, I was always worried. Worried about the brothers and sisters outside in the church. Worried about my family. Worried about my poor health. And then one day I thought, 'Why am I just worrying about all this, and not praying about it?' So I began to tell Jesus all my worries, and I was flooded with great peace. Then Jesus sent me a sister for fellowship. For a while she was in another room, and we sent notes to each other which was very dangerous. But then she was transferred into my room and we were together for two months. It was wonderful to read God's Word and pray together. Those in our cell could tell we were different.

"Just before I was released, she was sent off to another camp for a year. The last month I spent was very hard, full of ten-hour work days where we made plastic flowers for export. One week before I was released, the Public Security Bureau asked me to promise never to hold meetings in my home again. Praise God, I was able to tell them I would promise no such thing, and that they were welcome to read the Bibles they had confiscated from my home. I was still released."

Please pray for those in prison today as you read this story.

Sister Ruth

The fruitful leader

"But when they arrest you, do not worry about what to say or how to say it. At that time you will be given what to say, for it will not be you speaking, but the Spirit of your Father speaking through you." (Matthew 10:19-20)

Ruth sat down on the dirt floor. Her senses were revolted by the terrible stench of the cell. She could not remember anything that smelled as bad as this room – even the wooden buckets used to carry urine and 'night soil' to the fields for fertiliser. There was no toilet here, not even a hole in the corner. Nor was there any water supply.

She could feel the lice, spiders and cockroaches crawling on her. Blood-thirsty mosquitos were seemingly everywhere. And it was so dark she could not even see the faces of the other cell-mates. She slapped something crawling on her arm as she thought of her three children. With her husband Michael now in labour camp, the children were home all alone. Daniel was ten, Joseph eight and little Mary only five.

"Lord please take good care of my children," she prayed. "And also the young leaders of the house churches. Please don't let my imprisonment implicate them in any way."

Through the heavy darkness came a friendly voice, "Do you have any children?" It was as though they were reading her mind.

"Yes, three," she quietly replied. "Actually I had four children, but one is dead now."

"What happened?"

Ruth could not speak for a moment. Unseen tears slowly trickled down her round cheeks. "Lord, help me glorify you in everything I say," she silently prayed.

Suffering that purifies

Finally she began in a halting, wavering voice. "Peter was my eldest. Three years ago, when he was 11, the Red Guards came to search our home. There must have been a hundred of them in the search party. They already knew that my husband Michael and I were the leaders of a large number of house churches in this area. They kicked down the front door, tied up my husband and shaved both our heads.

"They pointed their rifles at our heads and demanded, 'Where are your Bibles? Where are your co-workers? Where do you hold your meetings?' We refused to answer so they began destroying our furniture and household belongings. Even the kitchen pots and pans. They dug up the floors and knocked down walls in their search.

"For three days and nights we were not permitted to eat, drink or sleep. Then they took our four children and lined them up on a bench. When they fell off from exhaustion, the Red Guards would beat them and stand them up on the bench again. Since my husband and I would not answer their questions, they began to interrogate the children. They asked, 'What do your parents do each day? Where do your mother and father hide their Bible?'

"The children also refused to answer. They knew that if we confess Christ before men, he will confess us before our Father in heaven. Whether you live or die, you must confess the Lord Jesus. But you must never reveal the name of a co-worker!

"They became more upset with the children and harshly demanded, 'Do you believe in the Communist Party or Jesus Christ?' Together the four children raised their hands and said, 'We believe in Jesus Christ!' The Red Guards were livid and knocked the children onto the floor with poles and stood them up again.

"This time they yelled, 'Why does your home not have a portrait or book of Mao Tze-tung nor any altar to him?' The children calmly replied, 'We don't worship idols! We only worship the God of creation who made heaven and earth.'

"Again they beat the children. Peter was dragged outside the house by the now enraged Red Guards. They beat him up so badly that his teeth were knocked out and he was bleeding all over. Then they threw his limp body in a pile on the floor. Not satisfied, they then turned on my husband. They put a card on him that read, 'The child of God who preaches Christianity...traitor... anti-revolutionary.' He was then hauled off to the regional hard labour camp for school teachers.

"Now I was left alone with the four children. Peter was lying on the floor, dying. There was no one to help me. All I could do was keep my eyes on Jesus. I took Peter to the hospital. The doctor said there was no hope since he was now vomiting blood from his mouth. I was told to prepare for his funeral and given the necessary certificate.

"The authorities allowed my husband a short leave from the labour camp to attend our son's funeral. When Peter saw his father, he was very happy. 'Mum and Dad,' he said, 'most people are dressed in black when they die but I want to be dressed in white so that I will be beautiful when I see God!' We tearfully agreed with him and knelt down and prayed with him that God's name would receive glory.

"Since it was winter time, the windows were all shut. But after we prayed, the windows opened and a gust of wind blew into the room and carried in some leaves. And the spirit of comfort came into our hearts. Peter whispered, 'Mum and Dad, Jesus has come to take me home to heaven. Goodbye!'

"I said, 'Goodbye, darling. We'll have a beautiful reunion someday. You go ahead. We'll all join you before long in the heavenly home.' His face was filled with joy when he went to be with the Lord at about quarter past one in the morning. Even the doctor was moved. He commented, 'I have never seen anyone die so peacefully!'

"When we arrived home, the three younger children rushed to us with excitement. 'We haven't slept yet because we saw a whole crowd of angels in our house. They had musical instruments and they sang to us. They said they were going to take Peter to heaven with them!'

"I told them, 'Your brother has already gone to be with Jesus.' They cried. He had loved them very much and they in turn loved him dearly."

There was a long silence. Ruth could hear sobs coming from all over the dark cell. Suddenly an angry voice cried out, "Curse those Red Guards! Why do they get away with this? I wish I could get my hands on their necks. They'd be the dead ones!"

"No, no," Ruth called out. "You mustn't hate them. That is a vicious cycle of bitterness. Jesus taught we must love even our enemies. I pray every day for those Red Guards – that they'll find Jesus. In the same way, I'll pray for all of you. You too are loved by Jesus."

There were slapping sounds everywhere as the cell-mates tried to scare away the hoards of mosquitos and other insects. "Hah," responded a cynical voice. "If Jesus loves me so much, why am I here in this filthy cell?"

Ruth began to explain how the filth of their cell was just like sin. It had alienated all people from a holy God. Only an acceptable sacrifice would bridge the gap between man and God. And the cross of Jesus provided that bridge. All they needed to do was confess their sin and ask Jesus to make them new people.

Again there was a long silence. Then one by one Ruth's cell-mates began to drop on their knees at her side and tearfully confess aloud their sinfulness and receive Jesus' gentle cleansing. "Thank you Lord. You really can turn everything into good!" Ruth praised God.

Practical love

In the morning, she could see the cell properly. It was indescribably dirty. The Lord prompted her to do something practical about the situation. She requested water and a bucket from the guards and amazingly they responded positively. Ruth got on her knees in that filthy cell and began to scrub. The guards were so impressed they got more water and buckets and assigned other prisoners to do the same.

When her cell was finally cleaned, Ruth asked if she could clean the other cells. The prisoners were astonished at her concern and practical love for them. As she scrubbed, she shared about her love for Jesus and taught them to sing. The favourite song was,

'Where Jesus is, Tis heaven there!' When other prisoners joined her, they sang while they worked and that terrible prison did become like heaven to them.

Ruth says, "We cleaned the prison until it was as clean as our homes. The authorities were so pleased that they opened the windows and installed lights. Now the inmates had a clean place to live and even better, Jesus was living in their clean hearts."

Confessing Jesus

The next day Ruth was taken out of the cell and told to confess her crimes. She replied, "What crimes?"

They said, "About your faith! Start at the age of eight!"

"I believed in Jesus even before the age of eight," she began. "The past five generations in my family all believed in him. They loved the Lord with all their hearts. When I was young, I had five major illnesses. The doctor said I was definitely going to die. But the Lord healed me and told me to share his Gospel."

She talked on for half of the day. The authorities were very touched by what she shared. But at noon they decided she needed another trial because she did not confess clearly enough. The Lord impressed on her to share about the last place at which she had preached. They took out paper and pen to record her confession. So she preached to them her sermon on the Second Coming of Jesus. The Holy Spirit worked in their hearts and they even asked her to sing them the song too.

The following day she was again taken from her cell. They said, "Yesterday you talked about Jesus! Today you must talk about something else. How many co-workers do you have? How many house churches? How did you begin?"

She replied, "I know Jesus. He is my Saviour and he can be your Saviour too. I don't know any other things. My co-workers have not committed any crime. And I have nothing to confess."

They insisted Ruth write out her confession. The Holy Spirit moved her to write 37 pages. She wrote about Jesus' birth, death and resurrection. She also wrote about heaven and hell. When she handed the cadre-in-charge her papers, he responded, "I asked you to write your confession but instead you have written a lengthy sermon. When I submit this you will surely die. I have no choice."

His superior read the pages one by one and concluded, "This person preaches outside and now she has put her preaching in writing to evangelise us. I sentence her to 20 years' imprisonment!"

That night they held a 'struggle' meeting against her. Four hundred prisoners and guards listened to her 'crimes'. The officials read aloud all 37 pages of her confession and the Holy Spirit worked in more hearts. Many prisoners repented in tears and received the Lord.

After 30 days had passed, the authorities announced to the prisoners that they were planning to release a selected inmate, regardless of sentence. They handed out ballots and instructed the prisoners to write the name of an inmate who had been best in behaviour and deserved to be released. They all wrote 'Ruth' on their ballots and miraculously she was discharged and soon walking home.

More miracles

Ruth's three children were overjoyed to see her. Her first question was, "Is there any rice left?" When she had been imprisoned a month earlier, there were only five catties of rice left. She had prayed for the Lord's provision for her children every day in prison.

Daniel's beaming response was, "Mum! Our rice container is overflowing!" And it really was, growing from five to over forty catties. Ruth's first job after prayers of thanksgiving with her children was to cook enough rice for the prisoners she had left behind that day – many now brothers and sisters in the Lord.

The very next day Ruth was out preaching the Gospel again. Overseeing the hundreds of house churches she had planted was a great responsibility. She did not take her leadership role lightly. But she also knew God would be in control.

Prison again

In less than a year she was re-arrested and taken to another prison. The day of her trial, the authorities chose a square large enough for 100,000 people. Many observers were brought from homes, schools, offices, and even re-education camps. Her husband, Michael, was also brought from his camp to witness her trial.

The prisoners were put on the large platform, interrogated and then sentenced – from five to 30 years. Several were given death sentences. A few fainted on the spot. For those without Christ, death is a tragic situation. The authorities concluded, "Anyone who dares to preach Christianity will receive the death sentence!" So Ruth was lined up on the grassy square with all the others sentenced to death by firing squad.

She calmly watched as the rifles were pointed toward her and breathed a quick prayer of committal to her Lord. The shots echoed in the square and everyone fell to the ground – except Ruth. It was a miracle of God's mercy!

That night she was again brought to an even higher stage for interrogation, sentencing and execution. The authorities treated her roughly this time dragging her up by the hair. They tied a rope around her wrists behind her back and then brought the rope up tight around her neck. It was then hung tautly from above. If she tried to relax her arms, the rope choked her neck. If she tried to relieve the pressure on her neck, it felt like her arms would break. Many people died from the pressure of this kind of hanging. It was far worse than being shot.

"May I say a few final words?" Ruth requested. The highest authority nodded assent. "When the Communists took over this land, I was only a 16-year-old student," she began. "I have not committed any crime against the nation, so why are you sentencing me to death?"

"We say there is no God," they replied. "You preach about God. Therefore you are public enemy number one and must be executed!" Ruth responded, "According to your Communist rules, there is freedom of religion."

"Why do you have to preach the Gospel?" they countered. She answered, "I have seen the Lord Jesus with my own eyes. I also had five incurable diseases and was told to prepare to die. When I met Jesus, he healed all my diseases. I carry the five doctor's certificates in my jacket pocket as a reminder. Jesus commissioned me to preach the Gospel! This is not hurting our nation."

No one responded so she began to share the Bible message. She started with creation and how Adam fell and God prepared a way for salvation. The message continued with the birth, ministry, death, resurrection, ascension and coming return of the Lord Jesus. She concluded with heaven and hell and judgement. Everyone was obviously deeply moved.

After coming down from the stage, Ruth was bleeding all over and had many internal wounds as well. The prison doctor gave her a very cursory check-up and signed a document that she was terminally ill and would die soon. This secured her release from the second imprisonment.

'Lord, send a Bible'

The next day she was back preaching again and visiting the house church leaders to encourage them! She was always distressed at the shortage of Bibles for the fast-growing churches. She continued to pray that God would perform a miracle and send them many. She loved to sing and wrote a special chorus to articulate their need:

> Lord, send a Bible for that's Your gracious light,
> True light and teaching and the bread of life.
> I know for sure that Your word will lead me home,
> Brighten the way all through my journey home.

In time, her fast-growing group of churches were to be the main recipients of Open Doors' 'Project Pearl' – one million Chinese Bibles delivered in one night at one location.

During her third imprisonment for preaching, Ruth was given a vision from the Lord. She saw thousands of missionaries from the West and the East working side by side digging a ditch. The ditch became bigger and longer after much hard work. Then water started to flow into it. It became the River of Life. She saw it flow first through all parts of China and after that into the whole world. The workers were very happy and their singing filled heaven and earth.

Today Ruth continues to work in evangelism to fulfil the vision…bearing fruit and waiting for her Lord to return.

"I tell you the truth, unless a kernel of wheat falls to the ground and dies, it remains only a single seed. But if it dies, it produces many seeds." (John 12:24)

Practical prayer point: Beatings…by Alex Buchan

Women make up over 70 per cent of China's Church – both official and unofficial. Unfortunately, the vast majority of them pay a heavy price to join that church. It is estimated that at least 40 per cent of these women face beatings from their husbands when they declare their allegiance to Christ, and five per cent are beaten so severely that permanent damage occurs.

In Henan province, a Christian wife was beaten severely with a piece of wood by her non-Christian husband. In Heilongjiang province, a Christian wife was whipped with a bamboo stick and then tied to a cart and paraded around the village. In Zheijiang province a husband sliced off an ear of his newly-converted wife. In Xiamen, Fujian province, two sisters who converted were nearly drowned by their husbands in a river. Their faces were held underwater until they lost consciousness. One was near death and only quick work from a passing doctor saved her life.

The phenomenon reflects the low status of women in Chinese society. Said one China researcher, "Chinese men view women as property rather than people, in much the same way as ancient Romans viewed slaves." When their wives become Christians, that very action challenges the entire social system at a stroke.

45

The husband feels challenged because his wife took a major decision without his say so, and interprets it as an act of defiance.

Please pray for all those who suffer beatings for Christ. It is touching to see how so many love to read the story of Jesus suffering his beating at the hands of Roman soldiers. Said a 65-year-old woman, whose Party member husband had abused her for 30 years, "The only reason I can keep going is the knowledge that Jesus went through for me first what I am now going through for him." She added, "He brought me life by his stripes, the least I can do is to bear some for him."

Open Doors International Vision Statement

We believe that all doors are open and that God enables his body to go into all the world and preach the Gospel. We therefore define our ministry as follows:

- To strengthen the body of Christ living under restriction or persecution by providing and delivering Bibles, materials, training and other helps, and encouraging it to become involved in world evangelism.

- To train and encourage the body of Christ in threatened or unstable areas, to prepare believers to face persecution and suffering, and to equip them to maintain a witness to the Gospel of Christ.

- To motivate, mobilise, and educate the Church in the free world to identify with and become more involved in assisting the Suffering Church, believing that when *"one members suffers, all the members suffer with it"* (1 Corinthians 12:26 NKJV).

How you and your church can make a difference

Prayer – the believers in persecuted lands live in a fierce spiritual battlefield. They need focused, intercessory prayer. Open Doors prayer magazines and newsletters provide you with daily prayer items to enable you to pray for these brothers and sisters and stand beside them in their struggle.

Bible Couriers – for decades, Open Doors has been helping believers carry Bibles and Bible study aids into the areas of greatest persecution. God uses ordinary people to take his Word to people living where faith costs the most. You can be one of them.

Adult and Children's Bibles – many persecuted believers have been beaten and imprisoned for their faith, yet don't have a Bible of their own. The young people in persecuted lands are special targets for false teaching and government control. Leaders know they must have control of the minds of the youth if they are to stop the spread of Christianity. Open Doors is providing the Church with special adult and children's Bibles that present the truth through words and pictures. Your generous gifts make this possible.

Leadership Training for Church Growth and Evangelism – most church leaders in persecuted lands have never had any formal training. Bible Schools either don't exist or have been destroyed. Open Doors works to fill this vacuum in these lands with Bible-based training tailored to the needs and culture of each area.

Your faith can equip and encourage the future leaders of our fellow believers who suffer for their faith.

For more information, write to:

Open Doors
PO Box 53
Seaforth
NSW 2092
AUSTRALIA

Missao Portas Abertas
CP 45371
Vila Mariana
CEP 04010-970
São Paulo
BRAZIL

Open Doors
PO Box 597
Streetsville, ONT
L5M 2C1
CANADA

Portes Ouvertes
BP 141
67833 TANNERIES
Cédex
FRANCE

Porte Aperte
CP 45
37063 Isola della Scala
Verona
ITALY

Open Doors
Hyerim Presbyterian
    Church
Street No 403
Sungne 3-dong
Kangdong-gu #134-033
Seoul
KOREA

Open Doors
PO Box 47
3850 AA Ermelo
THE NETHERLANDS

Open Doors
PO Box 27-630
Mt Roskill
Auckland 1030
NEW ZEALAND

Åpne Dorer
PO Box 4698 Grim
4673 Kristiansand
NORWAY

Open Doors
PO Box 1573-1155
QCCPO Main
1100 Quezon City
PHILIPPINES

Open Doors
1 Sophia Road
#06-11 Peace Centre
SINGAPORE 228149

Open Doors
Box 990099
Kibler Park 2053
Johannesburg
SOUTH AFRICA

Portes Ouvertes
Case Postale 267
CH-1008 Prilly
Lausanne
SWITZERLAND

Open Doors
PO Box 6
Witney
Oxon OX8 7SP
UNITED KINGDOM

Open Doors
PO Box 27001
Santa Ana
CA 92799
USA

You can visit the Open Doors website on www.od.org